CUTTING EDGE
TECHNOLOGY

Cutting Edge Transportation Technology

ReferencePoint
Press®

San Diego, CA

Other books in the *Cutting Edge Technology* series

CUTTING EDGE
TECHNOLOGY

Cutting Edge Transportation Technology

Barbara Sheen

ReferencePoint Press®

San Diego, CA

© 2017 ReferencePoint Press, Inc.
Printed in the United States

For more information, contact:
ReferencePoint Press, Inc.
PO Box 27779
San Diego, CA 92198
www.ReferencePointPress.com

LIBRARY OF CONGRESS CATALOGING-IN-PUBLICATION DATA

Names: Sheen, Barbara, author.
Title: Cutting edge transporation technology / by Barbara Sheen.
Description: San Diego, CA : ReferencePoint Press, Inc., [2017] | Series: Cutting edge technology | Includes bibliographical references and index. | Audience: 9-12.
Identifiers: LCCN 2016020639 (print) | LCCN 2016020976 (ebook) | ISBN 9781682820469 (hardback) | ISBN 9781682820476 (eBook)
Subjects: LCSH: Transportation engineering--Juvenile literature. | Transportation--Technological innovations--Juvenile literature. | Motor vehicles--Juvenile literature.
Classification: LCC TA1149 .S54 2017 (print) | LCC TA1149 (ebook) | DDC 629.04--dc23
LC record available at https://lccn.loc.gov/2016020639

Contents

Innovations in Transportation Technology

1903
The first powered, piloted airplane flies. The fabric-covered biplane with a wooden frame was invented by Americans Orville and Wilbur Wright.

3500 BCE
The wooden wheel is invented during the Bronze Age. Historians theorize that it was invented by the Tripolye people who lived in what is now Ukraine.

1869
The first transcontinental railroad in the United States is completed, making it possible for Americans to travel coast to coast via rail.

1807
The first commercially successful steamboat, the *North River Steamboat* built by Robert Fulton, is launched.

BCE ••• CE	1600	1700	1800	1900

1620
The first navigable submarine is built by Dutch inventor Cornelius Drebbel. It is propelled with oars.

1883
The first automobile powered by an internal combustion engine is developed by German inventor Karl Benz.

1783
French inventors Joseph-Michel and Jacques-Étienne Montgolfier launch the first hot air balloon.

1908
Henry Ford develops an assembly-line method of producing automobiles. This makes cars cheaper and more accessible to more people.

1914

American physicist Robert Goddard, the inventor of modern rocket ships, is awarded a patent for liquid fuel–powered rockets and for two- and three-stage rockets.

2011

Automobile manufacturer Tesla Motors releases the first commercially available electric-powered sports car. The car can reach a top speed of 130 miles per hour (209 kph).

2004

Space Ship I makes the first manned privately funded spaceflight. It wins a $10 million prize in the Ansari X Prize competition for the first nongovernmental organization to build and launch a reusable manned spacecraft.

2000

Japanese automaker Toyota releases the Prius, the first four-door electric-gas hybrid automobile, in the United States.

1910 ••• 1950 ••• 2000   2010

1939

The world's first turbo jet engine–powered aircraft, the Heinkel He 178, takes flight, beginning a new age in aviation.

2005

The world's largest passenger airplane, the Airbus A380, takes flight. It can carry 555 passengers.

2012

The Honda FCX Clarity, a hydrogen fuel cell–powered automobile, is available in California for lease only. The car costs about $1 million to manufacture.

2002

The first maglev train opens in Shanghai, China.

2015

SpaceX and Blue Origin each land a rocket in upright vertical position.

Changing the World

In 2015 the Dutch airline company KLM unveiled a design for a new type of aircraft known as the Advanced Hybrid Engine Aircraft Development, or AHEAD. AHEAD is equipped with two engines that are powered by clean-burning fuels. One runs on liquid hydrogen, while the other runs on biofuel. It has two sets of wings—a small pair on its nose and a large pair that is built into the plane's body. This gives AHEAD a curved shape. The design and the mounting of the aircraft's engines onto the back of the vehicle, rather than under the wings, improve airflow over the airplane. This reduces wind resistance, or drag, thereby increasing fuel economy. In fact, AHEAD is expected to be able to fly more than 8,700 miles (14,000 km) without refueling. That is about the distance from Australia to Kansas.

The unconventional location of the engines has another advantage. In traditional airplanes, engine noise is directed downward. The placement of AHEAD's engines on the back of the aircraft sends engine noise upward, reducing noise pollution on the ground. Overall, AHEAD is extremely aerodynamic, quiet, and environmentally friendly, putting it a step ahead of current aircraft. AHEAD is part of a long-term aircraft design study. It is expected to be operational by 2050.

Changing Technology

Vehicles like AHEAD are just one of many new technologies being developed to improve transportation. Transportation refers to the movement of people and things from one place to another. There are many forms of transportation, including wheeled and tracked vehicles, aircraft, spacecraft, and marine vessels. All forms of transportation are dependent on infrastructure such as highways, bridges, tunnels, airports, and seaports to move efficiently.

Humans have always depended on transportation systems to

Most of today's passenger aircraft, like the ones pictured here at an airport in the Netherlands, have engines mounted under the wings. The engines on the AHEAD plane, by contrast, will be mounted at the back of the craft, which will improve airflow and reduce noise on the ground.

move goods from where they are produced to markets where they can be sold and consumed. Transportation is vital to commerce. It also connects people and cultures, allowing for the exchange of ideas. As an article on the website Saving Communities explains, "All trade of wealth and productive labor involves transportation, whether it is the movement of goods or the movement of people from their homes to their jobs or their homes to the places where they shop. Trade is impossible without transportation, and complex trade is impossible without modern, mechanized transportation."[1]

Since transportation is so important to society, it has been the center of innovation for thousands of years. From the invention of the wheel to the development of self-driving cars, throughout history new technology has made it possible for people and goods to travel farther and faster than ever before. In fact, an individual who lived long ago would probably be amazed by the tremendous advances that have been made in transportation and how these advances have changed the world.

Before the Industrial Revolution, most early forms of transportation were fueled by human or animal power. Civilizations close to water relied on wind power to propel sailing ships. Travel was slow, dangerous, and expensive. Most people never ventured far from the town where they were born or came in contact with people and goods from distant cultures.

The invention of new technology in the form of the steam engine was instrumental in changing this. Although the ancient Greeks were the first to devise a working steam engine, it was not until the Industrial Revolution that steam engine technology was refined for practical use. With steam-powered ships and railroads in full operation by the middle of the nineteenth century, people and goods were able to travel farther and faster. In fact, a sea crossing that took five weeks in 1800 was reduced to eighteen days by the middle of the nineteenth century. By the end of that century, the same trip took about five days. Similarly, by 1890 steam-powered railroads were carrying millions of passengers and tons of cargo each year. Travel became cheaper and easier. Ordinary people were now able to seek work farther from home, socialize with people from other towns, see more of the world, and exchange goods, services, and ideas.

infrastructure

The basic structures and equipment, such as bridges, roads, and railroad tracks, that are needed for a transportation system to operate effectively.

The invention of the internal combustion engine, followed by that of the automobile in the late 1800s, further improved transportation. Once motor vehicles, trains, and ships were powered by internal combustion engines, travel time was reduced even more. Still newer technology led to the development of commercial aircraft and, later, jet engines. The latter made it possible for people to board an airplane on one continent and disembark on another in the same day.

Eventually, newer and better transportation technology produced globalization, a process in which marketplaces are interconnected and products, ideas, technology, and other aspects of culture are freely interchanged worldwide. And as economies became more connected, opportunities for growth and development also increased. Massachusetts secretary of transportation Stephanie Pollack explains, "Transportation is not important for what it is; transportation is important for what it does. Get people where they need to go and connect them to opportunity. Shape and support the economy of communities and regions."[2]

Safer, Cleaner, Faster

Although the development of new transportation technology has done much to improve society, it has also caused problems. For instance, the density of vehicles on roads and the speed at which those vehicles travel has led to about 1.2 million traffic-related deaths per year worldwide.

Another problem is pollution. All forms of transportation use energy for power, with fossil fuels like oil and coal most commonly used for this purpose. Burning fossil fuels releases harmful chemicals into the air, which can negatively affect people's health. It also emits greenhouse gases that climate scientists say contribute to global warming. Unwanted sound, or noise pollution, caused by motor traffic, aircraft, and mass transit systems is another transportation-related problem. Even new computer technology used in vehicles can cause problems related to cybersecurity and privacy issues.

Researchers are developing new technologies that address these and other problems. Although there is no way to foresee what the future holds, history suggests that new technology will continue to change transportation, and in turn, transportation will continue to change the world.

CHAPTER ONE

Powering Motor Vehicles

Currently more than 1 billion passenger cars travel the world's roadways, and according to the International Organization of Motor Vehicle Manufacturers, about 89 million new cars are manufactured each year. Most of the world's vehicles are powered by gasoline or diesel fuel. Both are derived from petroleum, which is a fossil fuel. Fossil fuels are nonrenewable resources, meaning that once petroleum reserves run out, they cannot be replaced. Currently about 85 million barrels of oil are consumed each day, approximately two-thirds of which is used to power transportation vehicles. Scientists estimate that at the current rate of usage, the world's oil reserves will be used up in about forty years.

Even if more oil reserves are discovered, powering vehicles with fossil fuels is problematic. Removing petroleum from the earth is a complex process that can damage area ecosystems. When fossil fuels are burned, they release into the atmosphere greenhouse gases such as carbon dioxide, which trap heat and are believed to contribute to global warming. Other toxins are also released that degrade air quality and cause respiratory problems for some individuals.

Powered by Electricity

To help solve these problems, scientists are developing environmentally friendly motor vehicles that are designed to cut down on fuel consumption and harmful emissions. Electric vehicles (EVs), which are powered solely by electricity and produce zero carbon emissions, fall into this category.

Outwardly most EVs look like gas-powered vehicles, and they usually have the same standard features as conventional cars. Although the most obvious difference is that EVs, unlike gas-powered vehicles, are silent, the most significant differences are found under the hood. Instead of a traditional gas engine, EVs

Although electric vehicles look similar to gas-powered vehicles, they feature electric motors that must be charged periodically. Here, an electric vehicle on display at a car show receives a charge.

have one or two electric motors. These are connected to a computerized controller, which transfers power from a battery to the motor. Just as gas-powered vehicles can run out of gas and must be refueled, an EV's battery must be recharged periodically. Depending on the vehicle, this is done either by plugging the EV into a standard electrical outlet or a special high-voltage outlet. Charging can take up to twelve hours. EVs get additional power from regenerative braking, a process in which kinetic energy is transferred to the battery when the driver steps on the brake pedal.

Electric vehicles have been around since the middle of the nineteenth century. Early battery technology, however, did not provide the vehicles with enough power to be practical. It was not until the twenty-first century that environmen-

kinetic energy

Energy derived from motion.

tal concerns, combined with the development of rechargeable lithium-ion batteries, spurred the development of modern EVs. Lithium-ion batteries come in different sizes and strengths, but even the least powerful can store and release a great deal of

Cold Weather and Electric Vehicles

When a connection is made between a battery's negative and positive terminals, a chemical reaction that creates an electric current occurs. Cold temperatures slow down the chemical reaction, reducing the strength of the current. Therefore, when outside temperatures fall below freezing, an EV or plug-in hybrid vehicle's range can drop by as much as 50 percent. In an effort to improve the performance of EV batteries at low temperatures, scientists at Pennsylvania State University are developing a self-heating lithium-ion battery.

The battery contains a tiny strip of nickel foil created through nanotechnology. One end of the foil is attached to the battery's negative terminal, while the other end extends outside the battery. When temperatures fall below freezing, a temperature sensor signals the battery to send electrons through the foil. This creates a new circuit between the battery's negative terminal and the external tip of the foil, which warms the battery. Once the battery is at 32°F (0°C), the temperature sensor signals the electric current flow to return to normal.

energy. An EV's travel range depends on the particular vehicle and the capacity of the battery. Most have a range of 80 to 100 miles (129 to 161 km). Some, like the Tesla X, which uses a super powerful battery, can go up to 257 miles (414 km) on a full charge. Even so, many drivers worry that the battery will run out of power before they reach their destination or a charging point. This concern led to the development of hybrid vehicles.

A hybrid vehicle is a cross between a traditional gasoline-powered vehicle and an EV. Hybrids use two or more power sources. Generally, these sources consist of a gasoline engine and two electric motors. A computerized controller under the hood determines when the vehicle is fueled by electricity and when it is fueled with gas. Conventional hybrids are powered by electricity when the vehicle is being driven at low speeds, such as in-town commutes, while a gasoline engine fuels the vehicle for long-distance, high-speed driving. The batteries, which are generally low capacity, recharge via regenerative braking. However, the newest type of hybrids, such as the Chevy Volt, offers a plug-in option. Plug-in hybrids are powered almost exclusively by electricity while still featuring a small gasoline engine for backup. As Mary Barra, CEO of General Motors, explains, "There are still people who say, 'but what happens when you run out of electric energy?' It's OK! You can go another couple of hundred miles on gas. Our Volt allows people who use it for short trips and recharge regularly to get an average 900 miles between gas fill-ups."[3]

Solving Problems

Despite advances in battery technology, EVs and hybrids have not yet been perfected. In fact, the batteries may still be the weak link. The amount of time it takes to fully charge a battery is one issue. A lithium-ion battery is made of various substances that, because of the differences in their composition, slow the flow of electricity through the battery. This is known as internal resistance.

To combat this problem, StoreDot, an Israeli company, is developing a new kind of battery called the FlashBattery, which is expected to be able to store enough energy for an EV to go about 300 miles (480 km) on a five-minute charge. The invention is made of organic substances created using nanotechnology, the manipulation of atoms and molecules to create tiny particles or systems about fifty thousand times smaller than the diameter of a human hair. Because these substances are so much alike, internal resistance is reduced, which in turn lessens the time it takes to charge the battery.

The company is already marketing a version of the FlashBattery for use with small electronics. Work on more powerful batteries suitable for motor vehicles is ongoing. If all goes well, the FlashBattery will make charging EVs and plug-in hybrids significantly faster in the future.

British researchers, too, are working on another way to charge EVs' and hybrid cars' batteries. They are developing roads capable of charging a vehicle's battery while it is being driven. In this technology, charging coils that generate electromagnetic fields are buried beneath the roads. EVs and hybrids are fitted with a special receiver that picks up the electromagnetic waves and converts them to electric power that is fed to the battery. The British government has committed the equivalent of about $700 million to advance this technology. Trials of the concept were scheduled to begin on special test roads in late 2016. If they are successful, the technology will be tested on working roads. Chief highways engineer for Highways England Mike Wilson explains, "Vehicle technologies are advancing at an ever increasing pace and we're committed to supporting the growth of ultra-low emissions vehicles on our England's motorways. . . . The off road trials of wireless power technology will help to create a more sustainable road network for England."[4]

Lightening the Load

Other new technology aims to increase the range and performance of hybrid vehicles by reducing their weight. Because hybrids contain gas and electric engines and batteries, they are heavy. Since it takes more force to move heavier vehicles, hybrids are not usually as nimble as lighter vehicles. With that in mind, the automobile manufacturer Volvo is developing a lightweight energy-storing body panel that could replace a lithium-ion battery. Designed to cover a car's frame, the panel is made of extremely strong, light, flexible plastic, along with carbon fibers that contain tiny batteries created through nanotechnology. The batteries would collect energy just like a large battery but would reduce a hybrid's weight by about 15 percent. According to Volvo, "The panels would capture energy produced by technologies like regenerative braking or when the car is plugged in overnight and then feed that energy back to the car when it's needed."[5]

Toyota is taking this technology a step further. It, too, is developing lightweight energy-storing panels for hybrid vehicles. These

electromagnetic

When a magnetic field is produced by a current of electricity.

panels, however, are made from a special type of plastic derived from ocean plants and are embedded with photovoltaic cells, the same cells that are used in solar panels. The cells gather, generate, and store solar energy to help power the car. Although neither this panel nor Volvo's has been perfected, in the future such cutting edge technology should significantly increase a hybrid vehicle's performance.

Fuel Cell Vehicles

Other innovators are taking a different approach: They are developing fuel cell vehicles (FCVs). These vehicles have an electric motor, a small lithium-ion battery, a stack of hydrogen fuel cells, and one or more fuel tanks. The tanks feed hydrogen to the fuel cells. When the hydrogen combines with oxygen pulled into the fuel cells from outside air, a chemical reaction occurs that produces electricity to power the motor. The lithium-ion battery, fueled through regenerative braking, is not used for propulsion, but rather provides the vehicle with additional power for acceleration. A computer decides when to use energy from the battery or the fuel cells.

Two FCVs, the Hyundai Tucson Fuel Cell and the Toyota Mirai, are available in the United States (although there are only

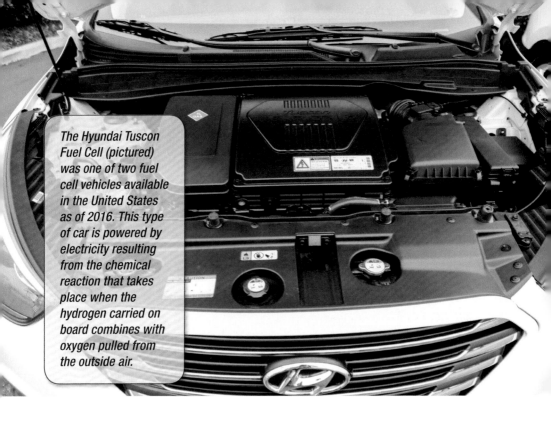

The Hyundai Tuscon Fuel Cell (pictured) was one of two fuel cell vehicles available in the United States as of 2016. This type of car is powered by electricity resulting from the chemical reaction that takes place when the hydrogen carried on board combines with oxygen pulled from the outside air.

twenty-two hydrogen fuel cell stations where drivers can refuel their FCVs in the nation). Both cars offer most of the features that conventional luxury vehicles provide and are just as quiet as an EV. And because hydrogen is flammable, the vehicles have a state-of-the-art safety system equipped with special sensors that sound alarms and seal valves and fuel lines in case of a hydrogen tank leak. Safety is also foremost in the design of the tanks. They are wrapped in carbon fiber, which is so strong that the tanks can absorb five times the crash energy of a steel fuel tank.

In appearance the Mirai is futuristic. Its most unusual feature is large twin vents located on each side of the front bumper. These are designed to pull large quantities of air into the fuel cells. Another interesting feature of the Mirai is an optional "out" port, which makes it possible to connect the car to an electric generator. With its hydrogen tanks filled, the Mirai could potentially supply an average home with power for a week, which might be useful in case of a blackout.

On the surface, FCVs appear to be extremely environmentally friendly; in fact, an FCV's only emission is water vapor. However, before hydrogen can be used for power, it must be separated from other chemicals. The most common way to do this is through a process known as steam reforming. In this process natural gas is treated with steam, which separates hydrogen molecules from the carbon oxides found in the gas. Although the hydrogen that is produced is a clean fuel, the process itself releases carbon dioxide pollution into the air.

Because hydrogen is such a promising fuel, scientists are looking into ways to produce it more cleanly. One method being studied involves harvesting hydrogen gas from green algae, which produce hydrogen during photosynthesis. If this can be accomplished, FCVs have the potential for being among the cleanest vehicles on earth, which is why Toyota Motor Corporation chair Takeshi Uchiyamada describes hydrogen fuel cell technology as a "societal and economic game-changer."[6]

Other Power Sources

Researchers are looking into other ways to fuel motor vehicles as well. One novel method that the automaker Peugeot Citroën, in partnership with the French government, has recently developed uses compressed air combined with a gasoline engine and special hydraulics (a system or tool operated by fluid) to power a car. The technology works in a similar way to that used in hybrid vehicles. However, instead of electricity, it uses compressed air for energy.

In this system a hydraulic pump and a piston compress air, which is stored in a tank. When the driver steps on the accelerator, the compressed air is released for power. The hydraulic pump also recovers energy from regenerative braking and transfers it into the air tank. The car can run on compressed air, gasoline, or a combination of the two. A computer determines the best method depending on the situation. Generally, gasoline is used at higher speeds, while compressed air is used between 60 percent and 80 percent of the

hydraulics

A term used to describe a system or tool moved or operated by fluid.

Much of the surface area of this solar-powered car, designed by scientists at the Massachusetts Institute of Technology, is covered with panels that collect energy from the sun to power it. The vehicle relies on stored energy when the sun is not shining.

time during in-town driving. The key benefits of this type of hybrid car over electric hybrids is that it is lighter weight, it has no batteries that need to be charged or replaced, and since air is free, the vehicle should be less expensive to operate.

Like air, solar power is also free. Researchers at a number of universities are involved in developing solar motor vehicles. These use photovoltaic cells to collect energy from the sun and turn it into electricity. The electricity in turn is stored in batteries and used to power an electric motor.

Solar vehicles must collect large amounts of solar energy in order to work, and therefore they must be designed to expose the greatest amount of surface area possible to sunlight. Many solar cars look more like aircraft than automobiles, with solar panels covering almost the entire surface area of their curved body. Such a car designed by scientists at the Massachusetts Institute of Technology, for example, resembles a flying saucer with wheels. The entire front of the car is covered with solar panels, which provide it with enough power to run all day at 55 miles per hour (88.5 kph) if the sun is shining. In the absence of sunlight, the car is powered with stored energy.

A pioneer in the development of solar-powered vehicles is SunRed, a Spanish motorcycle manufacturer that has built a prototype for a solar-powered motorcycle. Because motorcycles have a limited surface area on which to mount solar panels, harvesting enough energy to power one is a challenge. But the unique design of the SunRed motorcycle solves this problem. The motorcycle is covered with retractable solar panels. When the motorcycle is parked, the panels rise up to form a cocoon around it, making it look something like a snail. In this position the panels can fully charge the motorcycle's battery in about two hours. When the vehicle is driven, some panels fold down to make the driver's seat accessible, while others continue to cover the front and rear of the motorcycle and absorb solar energy.

Fuel from Waste

Still other automotive engineers are looking at another free source of energy—biogas. Biogas, a type of biofuel, is a naturally occurring gas that is produced when organic waste like dead animal and plant material, sewage, and manure break down in the absence of oxygen, as it does in landfills. Biogas is primarily made of methane and carbon dioxide, and it burns when combined with oxygen. It can also be compressed and used to fuel motor vehicles.

In nature organic matter releases carbon dioxide into the atmosphere as it decomposes, and it also releases some carbon when it is burned. For use as fuel, biogas is produced in airtight tanks so no carbon is released into the atmosphere, although it still releases some emissions when burned for fuel. However, this amount is about equal to the amount that would have been produced had the organic material been left to decompose naturally. Therefore, biogas is considered environmentally friendly.

prototype

A preliminary model of an object that is built to test an idea and that is used to develop other forms of the object.

A bus fueled by sewage and food waste, the Bio-Bus—also called the "poo bus"—is being tested in Bristol, England. It can carry forty passengers and looks like a traditional bus. If the vehicle proves to be successful, more will be built. As James Freeman, managing director of the bus company, explains, "The Bio-Bus has generated worldwide attention. . . . The very fact that it's running in the city should help to open up a serious debate about how buses are best fueled, and what is good for the environment."[7] Indeed, cutting edge technology is making it possible to power motor vehicles in cleaner, greener ways. It is likely that in the future all motor vehicles will be more environmentally friendly.

CHAPTER TWO

Safe and Smart Travel

At London's Heathrow Airport, self-driving taxis shuttle passengers from the parking lot to airport terminals. Sensors mounted on the vehicles and on the road guide the taxis along a pre-programmed route. In the United States, companies including Google, Uber, and General Motors, among others, are developing driverless cars that can travel on any route, just like traditional motor vehicles. These "connected" vehicles communicate electronically with each other and with infrastructure, which makes them less vulnerable to accidents caused by human error. All of these new vehicles share some common characteristics: They rely on computer technology to operate, and they are expected to make travel safer, easier, and more accessible.

Vehicle-to-Vehicle Connectivity

Drivers of motor vehicles are isolated from each other. If there is debris on the road or a traffic accident up ahead, there are few ways for drivers to alert each other. The US Department of Transportation (DOT) wants to change this. It has created a strategic plan that focuses on the development of intelligent transportation systems that use state-of-the-art technology to enable information sharing between vehicles. This is known as vehicle-to-vehicle (V2V) connectivity or communication.

V2V connectivity involves the use of a wireless network through which motor vehicles exchange information related to driving conditions at a rate of about ten times per second. This data includes information about vehicle speed and direction, braking, and traction control. For example, drivers would get a warning if another vehicle is merging into their blind side or if traffic down the road has slowed. With adequate warning, drivers can take necessary safety precautions or exit congested routes and take an alternate route. DOT estimates that V2V connectivity has the potential to reduce automotive accidents involving unimpaired drivers by 80 percent. According to the agency, "When cars share this information at such a fast rate, they can 'see' all of the vehicles around them, sense the possibility of a crash, and warn drivers to avoid the crash."[8] Moreover, information sent between vehicles would also be sent to transportation agencies to help officials better understand traffic flow and aid them in making decisions concerning traffic management.

The concept for V2V technology comes from the Internet of Things. This is a network that connects information from data-gathering sensors located in ordinary things like smartphones and household devices. The data is linked to a computer cloud and transmitted among the different things via wireless technology. V2V connectivity works in much the same way. In fact, the technology that V2V connectivity uses is sometimes referred to as the "Internet of cars." Bill Ford, chair of the Ford Motor Company, states, "Now is the time for all of us to be looking at vehicles on the road the same way we look at smart phones, laptops and tablets as pieces of a much bigger network."[9]

DOT's plan calls for every new motor vehicle to be equipped with multiple information-gathering sensors starting in 2020. The sensors rely on dedicated short-range communications, a Wi-Fi-like wireless communication system that allows vehicles to transmit information to each other about what they are doing. V2V communication would be part of a mesh network, in which information in the form of signals is passed between sensors in much the same way that runners in a relay race pass a baton. As a result, vehicles equipped with V2V technology could transmit, receive, and retransmit information to other similarly equipped vehicles even if they are miles apart.

In addition, as the technology progresses, the sensors would also be linked to a vehicle's brakes, accelerator, and steering systems, signaling it to slow down or steer around upcoming

connectivity

The use of a wireless network communication system that enables communication between vehicles, infrastructure, and personal communication devices.

Commuters around the world frequently cope with heavy traffic on their way to work. Vehicle-to-vehicle technology will make such drives safer by allowing cars to communicate with each other regarding possible roadway hazards.

roadside hazards without driver action. This autonomous driving feature would be especially useful in protecting distracted drivers, as well as enhancing the performance of self-driving vehicles.

Different methods of alerting drivers to incoming transmissions are being studied. Flashing colored lights that appear on a vehicle's instrument panel combined with an arrow pointing to the direction of the problem is one possibility. Information might also appear as a text message on a vehicle's navigation screen. Or a vehicle's front and rear lights could convey warnings by flashing rapidly and repeatedly. Warnings might also take the form of computer-generated voice messages sent through the vehicle's infotainment system.

For this process to be effective, most vehicles will need to have V2V capabilities. As *ExtremeTech* reporter Bill Howard explains:

> You don't need every car to be V2V equipped but you need a lot of them. . . . Early on in the V2V era, if your car has V2V and the car in front of you without V2V panic-brakes, you've got to be alert. . . . If both cars have V2V

and you're following closely, you'd be warned. . . . If you're farther back, one warning might be enough. In a pack of a dozen cars where three or four have V2V, the odds favor enough of them reacting to a traffic emergency so that all drivers will brake sooner. . . . What might have become a six-car pileup becomes two cars or none at all.[10]

Although the technology has many advantages, it raises security and privacy concerns among some individuals. V2V communication is designed to be anonymous and secure, but even secure systems are not perfect. If communication between vehicles could be intercepted, problems could result. A hacker with bad intentions could transmit bogus alerts, for example, sending drivers into risky situations, and there is also the danger that the technology might be used to illegally track vehicles. Researchers are taking these concerns into account in their work and are building extra layers of security and privacy protection into the technology.

autonomous

Not controlled by others.

Despite such reservations, eight automobile manufacturers working with scientists at the University of Michigan are currently testing twenty-five hundred V2V-equipped cars on a roadway in Ann Arbor. These companies, some individuals, and DOT believe that the safety benefits of V2V outweigh security concerns. In 2014 US secretary of transportation Anthony Foxx had this to say: "Safety is our top priority, and V2V technology represents the next great advance in saving lives. This technology could move us from helping people survive crashes to helping them avoid crashes altogether—saving lives, saving money and even saving fuel thanks to the widespread benefits it offers."[11]

Vehicle-to-Infrastructure Communication

As part of DOT's plan, connected vehicles will not only be able to communicate with each other, they will communicate with infrastructure—such as traffic lights and signals, roadways, and

Innovative Infrastructure

V2I connectivity is one way that vehicles and infrastructure can communicate with each other. Researchers are also looking into other ways in which roads can make driving safer and easier. In the Netherlands scientists are testing photoluminescent, or glow-in-the-dark, highways. The highways are treated with a substance that absorbs light during the day and glows neon green at night. Such treated roads provide better visibility for drivers than street lights and may eventually replace them.

Another idea under investigation is highways in which the roads themselves would serve as constantly changing interactive displays. Through the use of computer technology, traffic data would appear directly on the pavement, alerting drivers to their driving speed and informing them of traffic problems and road hazards. The technology would also make it possible for road signs to be constantly updated to reflect travel conditions. So, for example, the speed limit on a traffic sign would not be fixed. Instead, it would change depending on traffic conditions at a particular time. This would improve traffic flow.

Still another concept involves roads that would repair themselves. Scientists in the Netherlands have developed a form of concrete that contains a special bacteria that fills in cracks as soon as they appear. The bacteria are dormant until the cement cracks and water seeps in. The moisture activates the bacteria, causing it to excrete limestone, which seals the cracks.

bridges—embedded with sensors. This type of connectivity is known as vehicle-to-infrastructure (V2I) connectivity or communication. V2I communication works like V2V communication; for example, if road sensors detect an oil spill in the left lane, the sensors would transmit a message to approaching vehicles warning them to slow down and divert to other lanes. This same technology would make it possible for traffic signals to alert drivers to how much time they have before an upcoming traffic light will change, and what speed, within safe and legal limits, to drive to make all upcoming green lights. Similarly, parking meters could

Vehicle-to-infrastructure technology will enable cars to receive data from structures such as traffic lights, roadways, and bridges. One use of this technology will be traffic signals capable of alerting drivers to how much time they have before the light changes from green to red.

alert drivers to available parking spaces. This would save drivers time and help conserve fuel that would otherwise be consumed as they circle streets looking for a place to park.

Sensors on infrastructure would also be programmed to monitor the components of the structures themselves. This information would be transmitted to transportation agencies, providing managers with advanced warning about potentially critical safety issues such as broken traffic lights and crumbling roads.

At the present time, DOT is setting up a pilot V2V and V2I connectivity program in New York City. Ten thousand city-owned buses, cars, and other motor vehicles, as well as traffic signals along major avenues, are being equipped with the necessary technology. Data gathered through the program will help the agency determine the effectiveness of the technology.

Self-Driving Cars

Currently traffic accidents cause about 1.2 million deaths worldwide each year. Traffic accidents also cause injuries, permanent

Mcity

To ensure public safety, before large numbers of high-tech vehicles like autonomous cars or connected vehicles can be driven on actual roads, they must be tested in a controlled environment. At the same time, for the tests to be valid, the simulated environment and the situations the vehicles face should be as realistic as possible. This presents an interesting challenge.

Experts at the University of Michigan–Ann Arbor, working with the Michigan Department of Transportation, have created a unique test facility to meet this challenge. Known as Mcity, the test facility covers 32 acres (13 ha) on the university's campus. According to an article on the university's Mobility Transformation Center website, "Mcity simulates the broad range of complexities vehicles encounter in urban and suburban environments. It includes . . . roads with intersections, traffic signs and signals, sidewalks, benches, simulated buildings, street lights, and obstacles such as construction barriers."

The infrastructure is equipped with V2I communication technology. Also included on the streets are mechanized pedestrians, mechanized bicycles, and fixed and movable buildings. All types of traffic signals and signs are part of Mcity, as are crosswalks, lane delineators, and bicycle lanes. There are multiple curves in the roadway, off-ramps and on-ramps, a roundabout, tunnels, and a railroad crossing.

A number of auto manufacturers are taking advantage of Mcity to test advanced technology. For safety and confidentiality reasons, Mcity is not open to the public.

Mobility Transformation Center, "Mcity Test Facility." www.mtc.umich.edu.

disabilities, and financial losses. V2V and V2I connectivity have great potential to reduce traffic accidents, as do self-driving vehicles. These are vehicles in which people indicate where they want to go via a touch screen or voice activation, and the car takes care of the rest. No one in the vehicle is expected to control it. Egil Juliussen, an analyst for IHS Automotive, a firm that studies transportation trends, predicts: "Accident rates will plunge to near zero for SDCs [self-driving cars]."[12] In addition, self-driving cars would increase transportation access for disabled and elderly individuals who are not able to drive.

Also known as a driverless or autonomous car, a self-driving car is a robotic motor vehicle that, through cutting edge technology, can sense its surroundings and drive itself without human assistance. Robots are machines that are programmed to perform complex actions autonomously. They are directed in whole or in part by a computer and have sensors that allow them to obtain information from their environment.

Driverless cars are controlled by an onboard computer. They rely on hundreds of sensors located all over the vehicle, specialized software, Global Positioning System (GPS) technology, radar, a 360-degree camera, and a laser scanner, among other tools, to operate. Although the technology varies among auto manufacturers, a key part of self-driving-vehicle technology is a laser scanner that is mounted on the vehicle's roof or hood. When the vehicle is running, rotating laser beams emitted by the scanner take more than 1 million measurements per second of the vehicle's surroundings. These measurements are used to generate detailed three-dimensional maps of the environment. Moving objects such as pedestrians and other vehicles are shown on the maps, which are stored in the onboard computer along with preloaded high-resolution maps of the world. In addition to typical map features, the preloaded maps indicate the location of stationary objects such as traffic lights and crosswalks. Special software combines the two maps, which the computer uses for navigation purposes. This makes it possible for a driverless car to know where it is and what is going on around it at all times. At the same time, the camera and sensors gather additional information, which the computer also uses to help in navigation.

Other components control the car's ability to brake, accelerate, steer, and park. These utilize existing smart technology such

> ## lane-keeping system
>
> **A mechanism that warns a driver when the vehicle starts to move out of its lane.**

as self-parking systems, lane-keeping systems, adaptive cruise control, and automatic braking systems. "We have moved to cars that have millions of lines of code and advanced systems that will think about where you want to go and will change the brakes and steering to allow you to actually get there. So we're far along on the spectrum of automation,"[13] explains Bryant Walker Smith, a Stanford University fellow studying legal issues related to autonomous vehicles.

The best way to combine all these components and data has not yet been fully established. As Lawrence Burns, a consultant for Google's self-driving car program, explains, "The real secret sauce of all of this is what we call sensor fusion. How do you fuse together what the laser is seeing, what the radar is seeing, and what the camera is seeing, with the databases that you have already, and be very, very confident that what you're instructing the car to do is the right thing?"[14] V2V and V2I connectivity will help with this process. Sensors on driverless vehicles can use data transmitted from other vehicles and infrastructure to help predict where other cars will be, enabling the computer to make better driving decisions.

> **adaptive cruise control**
>
> **A form of cruise control that slows down and speeds up automatically to keep pace with the car ahead.**

Depending on the particular make and model of the vehicle, driverless cars may look like traditional sedans or they may be small two-passenger vehicles. Most will be fueled with electricity. Some automobile manufacturers are designing self-driving vehicles equipped with a steering wheel and brake and acceleration pedals for a human driver to use in case of an emergency, while others insist these devices are unnecessary.

Autonomous and Semiautonomous Vehicles

Before driverless vehicles become a common sight, a number of obstacles must be overcome. As with V2V technology, there are security issues. In fact, in 2015 computer-savvy researchers at

Wired magazine hacked into a computer-controlled communication program in a moving Jeep, disabling the vehicle. This showed how easy cyberattacks on computerized vehicles can be. Other issues involve the law. Most nations, including the United States, have laws that prohibit hands-free driving. Such laws will have to be changed in order for driverless cars to be legal.

Despite its great advances, driverless technology is not yet ready for mass market use. However, the technology has progressed far enough for companies such as Audi, Mercedes-Benz, Nissan, and Google to perform successful tests of self-driving car prototypes. In fact, Google's self-driving cars have successfully driven more than 500,000 miles (804,672 km) under a wide range of driving conditions. If tests continue to go well, automobile manufacturers estimate that driverless motor vehicles could be on the market by 2020.

In the meantime, researchers are hoping to bridge the gap between conventional vehicles and driverless vehicles with semiautonomous vehicles. Many late-model cars are already equipped with one or more driver-assistance systems that let the cars do more of the driving. However, according to the National Highway Traffic Safety Administration (NHTSA), having one or more driver assistance programs does not make a vehicle semiautonomous. To clarify the difference between traditional, semiautonomous, and driverless vehicles, the NHTSA developed a classification system that scores vehicles based on their level of autonomy, with vehicles having no automation ranking at level zero and driverless cars ranking at level four. Semiautonomous vehicles are rated level three. By the NHTSA's definition, "a Level 3 vehicle can handle all driving functions at the driver's discretion. . . . [However] the driver is expected to be available for occasional control, but with sufficiently comfortable transition time."[15] For example, at the touch of a button, semiautonomous cars can drive and park themselves. When the driver takes over, the vehicles assist the driver by centering themselves in highway lanes and adapting cruise control, among other tasks. As of March 2016, level three vehicles have not yet reached the mass market. But Tesla, Nissan, BMW, and General Motors expect to have such vehicles

A semiautonomous Freightliner truck travels down a road in California. These trucks can drive themselves on highways in daylight and fair weather, but a human driver must take over amid other driving conditions.

ready for global markets soon. And Freightliner, a truck manufacturer, tested a semiautonomous big rig known as the Inspiration in Nevada in 2015. The truck can drive itself on highways in daylight and fair weather but requires a human driver to take over under other driving conditions.

Similarly in 2016 six European truck manufacturers tested platoons of semiautonomous trucks on public roads in various cities throughout Europe. *Platooning* is a term used for convoys of vehicles that closely follow each other. The first vehicle serves as the leader. Using V2V and self-driving technology, the other vehicles follow the leader's movement, changing direction and speed whenever the lead vehicle does so. A similar concept is expected to be used in driverless cars. In this scenario, groups of cars driving a similar route would travel in groups known as flocks. The cars would move as one unit, with all the members of the flock taking cues from the leader. This would make it easier for driverless cars to navigate and would reduce traffic jams.

Although such a situation may sound like science fiction, semiautonomous and driverless cars, along with V2V and V2I connectivity systems, are key parts of the future of transportation. In fact, IHS Automotive predicts that by 2035, 54 million autonomous vehicles will be on the road worldwide. As Peter Sweatman, director of the University of Michigan Mobility Transformation Center, explains: "We believe that this transformation to connected and automated mobility will be a game changer for safety, for efficiency, for energy, and for accessibility. Our cities will be much better to live in, our suburbs will be much better to live in. These technologies truly open the door to 21st century mobility."[16]

CHAPTER THREE

High-Speed Public Transportation

It takes about six hours to drive from San Francisco to Los Angeles. If there are problems on the road, the 381-mile (613 km) journey can take even longer. And many of the vehicles on the road emit pollutants and greenhouse gases into the air. To make trips like this easier, faster, and more environmentally friendly, a variety of high-speed public transportation systems are in development. In fact, the California High-Speed Rail Authority wants to build a high-speed rail system that would connect a number of California cities. If the project is built, it could reduce travel time between San Francisco and Los Angeles to less than three hours. As Terry Ogle, the project's director of design and construction, explains, "California needs another transportation alternative. California's population is expected to grow by 25 percent over the next 30 years. That means by 2050, 50 million people will live in California. Anyone living or visiting LA or the Bay Area knows how congested the traffic is now; imagine what it'll be like with 50 million people trying to get around."[17]

High-Speed Trains

High-speed trains, also known as bullet trains, are a form of rail transportation that operates at faster speeds than traditional trains. Although there is no worldwide standard definition of a high-speed train, the International Union of Railways defines one as being capable of reaching speeds of at least 155 miles per hour (250 kph). Even though this sounds very fast, some of the most rapid high-speed trains can actually reach a maximum speed of about 236 miles per hour (380 kph).

High-speed rail transportation is not new; the world's first high-speed rail system began operation in Japan in 1964. Today high-speed rail lines operate throughout the world, with China

A high-speed train arrives at a station in Japan. Although high-speed rail lines are common in many other countries, there is only one in the United States. It links Boston, Massachusetts, with Baltimore, Maryland.

having the most extensive network on earth. As of 2016 there was only one high-speed rail line in the United States. Known as the Acela Express, it linked cities from Boston, Massachusetts, to Baltimore, Maryland.

Over the years advances in high-speed rail technology have made it possible for the trains to travel faster and farther than ever before. Cutting edge technology currently in development has the potential to change high-speed rail systems even more. Some interesting developments involve powering the trains. It takes a lot of power to move high-speed trains, which are traditionally fueled by electricity. Some high-speed train lines have their own electric grids, while others obtain electricity from national electric grids.

Although very few high-speed trains consume fossil fuels, many of the power grids that fuel them rely on fossil fuels to generate electricity. To avoid this and thereby make high-speed trains as environmentally friendly as possible, Solar Bullet, an American company, is looking into using solar energy to power a proposed high-speed rail line that would connect Phoenix and Tucson, Arizona. The company's researchers envision installing tracks connected to overhead canopies made up of solar panels. Photovoltaic cells in the panels would capture energy from the sun and convert it to electricity, which would be transferred to the tracks to power the train. The developers think the panels will generate enough electricity to power a train running at a speed of 220 miles per hour (354 kph).

The concept is still in development and faces a number of hurdles. One concern involves cleaning and maintaining the panels. Although Arizona receives plenty of sunshine, the state is subject to violent windstorms. Unless the panels are cleaned frequently, they could become coated with dust, interfering with their ability to do their job. Researchers are looking into different methods to handle this problem.

In the meantime, other nations are also experimenting with using solar energy to help power high-speed rail lines. Italy already uses solar energy to run the air-conditioning on some of its high-speed trains. And Belgium has installed sixteen thousand solar panels on the roof of a train tunnel, covering an area about the size of eight soccer fields. Belgian Railways predicts that the panels will generate enough power to operate four thousand trains per year entirely with solar energy.

Other researchers are looking into harnessing wind energy to power high-speed trains. For example, two industrial engineers, Qian Jiang of China and Alessandro Leonetti Luparini of Italy, have developed a device known as a T-Box, which is shaped like a cylinder with air vents on each side. The plan is to install the device between the cross ties of train tracks. When a train passes over a T-Box, the wind it generates enters the device through the vents, driving tiny turbines inside to produce electricity. It would take about 150 T-Boxes to cover 0.62 miles (1 km) of track.

evacuated

Having all the air removed, creating a vacuum.

As with solar panels, keeping the T-Boxes clean presents a challenge. Dust and debris, as well as grease from the trains, could clog the device's vents, reducing its ability to collect wind energy. Further research will likely produce ways to solve this problem.

China's Elevated Buses

China, with its huge and growing population, faces many public transportation challenges. Chinese scientists are developing a unique form of transportation, a bus network in which buses drive over cars and trucks on slightly modified roads. The huge buses, which straddle two lanes of traffic, look like an open-mouthed whale. Conventional vehicles would move through the open mouth, while bus passengers sit above it. This would make it possible for the buses to bypass traffic congestion and make scheduled stops without disrupting automobile traffic below.

The buses would roll on stilt-like legs along small tracks built into the sides of existing traffic lanes. Or they could run on regular tires. In this scenario the buses would be self-driving, programmed to follow painted lines on the sides of existing roads. Passengers would board the buses from elevated bus stops. Where elevated stops could not be built, passengers would board and exit the buses using built-in ladders.

The buses would be hitched together like trains in groups of four, allowing them to transport about twelve hundred passengers at a time. They would be powered by electricity, which would be supplemented by solar panels on the roofs of the buses. The vehicles would not need to be plugged in. Charging stations would be built along the bus routes in such a way that the buses would always make contact with the charging posts, thereby continuously being recharged.

Floating on Air

Another form of high-speed rail transport uses electromagnetic force to propel trains at speeds of about 310 miles per hour (500 kph). This method is known as magnetic levitation, and the superfast trains that rely on this system are known as maglev trains. Although maglev technology is not brand new, other cutting edge technology depends on it.

Maglev technology is based on the principle that magnets, depending on the position of their poles, either attract or repel each other. Opposite poles attract, while like poles repel each other. In maglev technology, electromagnetic coils that run along special steel tracks known as guideways produce a magnetic field that repels electromagnets located on the underside of train cars. Depending on the particular maglev system, the repelling force lifts train cars from 0.30 to 3.9 inches (1 to10 cm) above the guideway. As a result, the train literally floats on a cushion of air and in most cases does not need wheels. This eliminates friction that would normally occur when a moving vehicle makes contact with the ground.

Electromagnetic power that accelerates and decelerates the train comes from a special motor known as a linear synchronous motor that is built into the guideway. The conducting coils in traditional motors are arranged in a continuous loop, but the conducting coils in a linear motor are laid flat—allowing an electric current to pass through them in a straight line. The speed of the train is automatically controlled by the amount of electric power fed to the coils. Sam Gurol, director of transportation programs at General Atomics, a US company involved in developing new maglev technology, explains: "It operates similar to a wave coming towards the shore. That wave is not water, but electromagnetic. The surfer [in this case, the train] rides the wave."[18]

At the present time, only three countries—China, Japan, and Germany—have operational maglev systems. But a new state-of-the-art maglev system known as SkyTran may soon be built in Israel. This is a rapid-transit system in which passenger vehicles called pods travel underneath an elevated maglev track. Magnets on top of the cars and the bottom of the track create a powerful magnetic field that keeps the pods suspended. Electromagnetic energy accelerates and decelerates the vehicles. The pods look like wingless jet planes; each can carry two passengers and travel at an estimated 150 miles per hour (240 kph).

The system is driverless, following a preprogrammed route. Passengers select among various destinations by pressing a button in the pod. Then the pod heads directly to that destination without making other stops. If SkyTran is built, it will become the first aerial maglev public transportation system in the world. In the

In the rapid-trans SkyTran system (pictured), passenger vehicles called pods travel at speeds up to 150 miles per hour below an elevated maglev track. Magnets on top of the cars and the bottom of the track create a powerful magnetic field that keeps the pods suspended.

meantime, maglev technology is being used in the development of other cutting edge transportation systems.

"Space Travel on Earth"

Maglev technology is central to a new mode of high-speed urban and long-distance transport that is currently being studied. This system, which is known as evacuated tube transport, pairs vehicles known as capsules or pods with evacuated tubes. These are tubes in which the air has been permanently removed, creating a vacuum. The tubes, which are about 5 feet (1.5 m) in diameter, can be built of any material capable of holding a vacuum, such as concrete, steel, or plastic.

Each capsule is about the size of a midsize car and can hold six passengers or 800 pounds (363 kg) of cargo. The capsules are suspended inside the tubes using special superconductive magnets. Linear motors integrated into the tubes accelerate the capsules.

Since the tubes are airless, there is no air resistance. And since the capsules do not need wheels, there is no rolling resistance in the form of friction. Consequently, energy consumption is low, and the capsules can move at incredibly fast speeds. As an article on the *Gizmag* website explains:

> Anyone who has spent time on a fast motorcycle knows that even without any wind, the air itself is a brutally powerful force working against your engine as you get up above 125 mph (200 km/h). In fact, air resistance is the number one problem to combat as speeds increase. Airliners have to fly 40,000 feet up in the air to take advantage of the reduced drag you get when the air thins out a bit. . . . Take air resistance and rolling resistance away by operating in a vacuum and magnetically levitating your vehicle, and you're eliminating the biggest two hurdles to achieving extremely high speeds. And once you reach your top speed, you simply stop accelerating, apply no further energy, and coast. You lose very little speed until you reach your destination, at which point, you can slow your vehicle down electromagnetically and recapture almost all the energy you put in to speed it up.[19]

rolling resistance

The force resisting motion when an object rolls on a surface.

A system similar to regenerative braking in hybrid automobiles allows the energy to be recaptured.

Since individual capsules could be launched every twenty-six seconds, the system has the potential to move thousands of pounds of cargo and/or thousands of people per day. To accommodate passengers, the capsules will have pressurized air just as airplane cabins do. Passengers would enter and exit the capsules at airlocks in stations built along the route. This would allow for transfer without letting air into the tube.

Today's technology allows for speeds of about 400 miles per hour (644 kph). But researchers predict that as the technology is refined, speeds could reach 4,000 miles per hour (6,437 kph). This would make it possible to travel from New York to China in about two hours or go around the world in about six hours. In fact, Evacuated Tube Transport Technologies, an international consortium of scientists developing the technology, calls this type of travel "space travel on earth."[20]

Although not actually as fast as space travel, evacuated tube transport has the potential to move more passengers and cargo more rapidly than jet airplanes. The infrastructure could be built anywhere, even under the sea. Researchers envision the tubes forming a network like present-day freeways. The capsules would run along programmed routes, eliminating the need for a driver. To avoid scheduling delays, local lines and long-distance lines would have separate maglev tubes.

consortium

A coalition or association of two or more businesses, individuals, and/or institutions working to achieve a common goal.

As of 2016 no mass transport evacuated tube systems had been built. But Daryl Oster, the founder of Evacuated Tube Transport Technologies, envisions building a 14,500-mile (23,335 km) worldwide tube network that would go from New York to London via Alaska, China, India, and Europe. It would connect major cities and production centers and would cost significantly less to build than high-speed rail systems or freeways. Although the idea of traveling in a vacuum tube may sound more like science fiction than reality, with more research it is quite possible that evacuated tube transport systems will soon be zooming travelers all over the world.

Hyperloop

In 2013 Elon Musk, the CEO of Tesla Motors and SpaceX, put forward a concept for a new form of high-speed transportation known as a hyperloop. Like evacuated tube transport, it involves capsules traveling through tubes. However, although some of the air would be removed from the tubes, they would not be evacuated. Instead, air pressure in the tubes would be equivalent to

String Transport

Building the infrastructure for a high-speed rail system is very expensive. To help make high-speed rail more affordable, Russian scientist Anatoly Unitsky has developed a string transport system. The system consists of two steel or concrete rails suspended from towers anywhere from 10 to 98 feet (3 to 30 m) above the ground. High-tension steel wires, on which trains travel, run through the middle of the rails. The rigidity of the wires eliminates any sags or bumps, making for a smooth and fast ride. In fact, Unitsky predicts that trains could travel at speeds of more than 310 miles per hour (500 kph) on the high wires.

The system is designed to be both hurricane and earthquake proof. Because it requires less material than traditional high-speed rail lines, it will cost an estimated three to ten times less to build than a traditional high-speed rail line. Unitsky hopes to build a test installation in Australia in the future.

that found at an altitude of 150,000 feet (45,720 m). At this level, air resistance would be reduced but not eliminated. To counteract air resistance in the front of the capsule, the system uses an electric compressor fan mounted on the outer nose of the capsule. Its job is to transfer high-pressure air from the front of the capsule to the rear of the vehicle. The compressor is powered by an onboard electric motor fueled by more than three thousand batteries.

Some of the onrushing air would be directed to air casters located on the bottom of the capsule. An air caster is a type of device that uses pressurized air to create an air cushion that can lift and move heavy loads. The capsules would be suspended on this cushion in much the same way that pucks are suspended on an air hockey table. Linear motors located in the tube would accelerate and decelerate the capsules. Solar panels on the tube would help power the motors.

Hyperloop would be fast, reaching speeds of about 760 miles per hour (1,223 kph), but not as fast as evacuated tube transport.

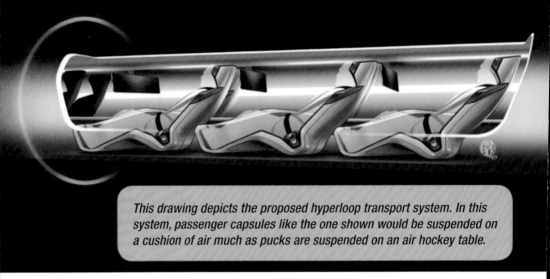

This drawing depicts the proposed hyperloop transport system. In this system, passenger capsules like the one shown would be suspended on a cushion of air much as pucks are suspended on an air hockey table.

The capsules would be larger, holding twenty-eight passengers each. The infrastructure would be built above ground, with the tubes set atop pylons that could run alongside major highways. Special tubes could transport automobiles. This would allow passengers to load their cars onto the hyperloop and travel with them to their destination.

Musk envisions hyperloop as a public transportation system that will be built to connect cities no more than 900 miles (1,448 km) apart. For greater distances, Musk thinks supersonic air travel would be more practical. Neither Musk nor his companies are directly involved in developing a hyperloop. But they are engaged in promoting the concept. In fact, to further the development of hyperloop technology, SpaceX sponsored a 2015–2016 hyperloop pod design competition in which teams of scientists, students, and other interested individuals were asked to design a hyperloop capsule. From these designs, thirty teams were chosen to build working prototypes. They planned to test the prototypes on a specially built 1-mile-long (1.6 km) track in California in late 2016. Musk hopes the competition will raise public interest in the technology and help spur the development of an actual hyperloop.

In fact, a number of companies and organizations are currently looking into developing a hyperloop. Although it may be many years before an actual system is built, hyperloop and other high-speed public transport systems have the potential to change the way people and things are transported. As Dirk Ahlborn, the CEO of Hyperloop Transportation Technologies, said in a 2015 talk, "How would your life be if you could travel 600 km in half an hour with a ticket price of $30? If we achieve that, we really change the way we live."[21] Indeed, it is likely that in the future high-speed transportation systems will allow passengers to zoom around the world with ease.

CHAPTER FOUR

Marine Vehicles

Marine transport is one of the oldest and most widely used forms of transportation. About 90 percent of the world's trade by volume is carried by large ships. Marine vehicles also transport people. The development of new high-tech marine vehicles ensures that this ancient form of transportation keeps moving into the future.

Green Ferries

Large ships use tons of diesel fuel every day, which results in a massive output of carbon emissions. Their giant engines also emit pollutants that can negatively impact the health of people who breathe them in. And the risk of environmental contamination from oil spills cannot be overlooked. Ferries that run anywhere from ten to twenty-four hours a day, seven days a week, are particularly fuel hungry. To help make ferries more environmentally friendly, engineers and scientists at the Sandia National Laboratories in New Mexico are partnering with San Francisco's Red and White Fleet ferry line to develop a hybrid hydrogen fuel cell/electric-powered ferryboat. It would work much like a hybrid hydrogen fuel cell/electric car. And, as with hydrogen fuel cell cars, its only emission would be water vapor. Says Tom Escher, president of the Red and White Fleet, "Everyone is talking about reducing emissions by 20 percent, 40 percent or more. I thought, 'Why not do away with emissions altogether? . . . I want to ride across the San Francisco Bay on a quiet, fast boat with no emissions."[22]

The prototype ship, which has not yet been built, has nonetheless already been named the *SF-BREEZE*, which stands for "San Francisco Bay Renewable Energy Electric vessel with Zero Emissions." Researchers initially considered converting an existing ferry into the *SF-BREEZE*. However, because onboard hydrogen fuel cells and tanks are quite a bit heavier than a traditional internal combustion engine, replacing a conventional engine on

Traditional ferries like this one consume tons of diesel fuel per day and expel vast amounts of carbon emissions. To solve these problems, scientists are attempting to develop a cleaner type of ferry powered by electricity and hydrogen fuel cells.

an existing ship with hydrogen power would reduce the ship's speed. So researchers decided to build a brand-new ship that can hold this extra weight without reducing the vessel's speed. In fact, the goal is to make the *SF-BREEZE* faster than conventional ferries. As Joe Pratt, the project's lead mechanical engineer at Sandia National Laboratories, explains: "If you are trying to achieve speed, boat weight is important. Fuel cells and hydrogen are heavier than existing diesel engines and fuel, so the question becomes can you build a boat powered by hydrogen fuel cells that is both large and fast enough?"[23]

A preliminary study indicates that building such a ship is indeed possible. The Elliott Bay Design Group, a private naval architecture firm working with the US Coast Guard and the American Bureau of Shipping, is slated to design the vessel. However, no specific design has yet been developed.

Keeping the ship fueled is another hurdle. It is estimated that the new ship will consume about 2,204 pounds (1,000 kg) of hydrogen per day. In comparison, an average fuel cell car uses

High-Tech Cruising

An estimated 20,335,000 people travel on cruise ships each year. In an effort to entice passengers, cruise lines are constantly updating their fleets. For example, from 2014 to 2016, the Royal Caribbean International cruise line launched three new ships that use a wide range of state-of-the-art technology to help ensure that guests enjoy their cruise. Passengers are issued wristbands that operate through wireless technology. The bands provide the wearer with information about the ship, track any expenses the wearer incurs on the ship, track the wearer's schedule (covering things like dining reservations and shore excursions), and also serve as a room key. Passengers can text each other and make changes to their schedules using a special smartphone app or at stations located throughout the ship that interact with the wristbands.

State-of-the art technology also controls robots that serve as shipboard bartenders, while other dancing robots interact with live dancers as part of a stage show. New technology is also used to provide passengers staying in cabins without balconies with a live stream of outside views. The views are displayed on a large LED screen mounted inside the cabin. Other technology allows passengers to take a fifteen-minute ride in a glass pod suspended about 300 feet (91 meters) above the ocean. The pod is powered by a massive hydraulic arm and offers riders 360-degree views.

about 11 pounds (5 kg) of hydrogen per week. To keep the vessel fueled, researchers propose building a hydrogen fueling station capable of dispensing 3,306 pounds (1,500 kg) of hydrogen per day on the dock. Such a facility would be both the largest hydrogen fueling station in the world and the first to serve both land and marine vehicles, because hydrogen-fueled cars and buses would also be able to use it. Although the project does not have a time line, a study to determine its feasibility is underway, and Escher is optimistic that both the ferry and the fueling station will be built.

In the meantime, an all-electric ferry is operating in Norway. Built to test the practicality of such a vessel, the ferry has so far passed the test. The vessel, which entered service in 2015, currently travels a 3.6-mile (5.8 km) route thirty-four times per day carrying both cars and passengers between two fjord villages. Each trip takes about twenty minutes and uses about 150 kilowatt hours of electricity.

Before the vessel could be launched, researchers had to figure out how to keep it charged so that it would not run out of power before reaching its destination. Their solution was to put two electric motors powered by lithium-ion batteries on the vessel, which provide it with 1,000 kilowatt hours of power. This is enough electricity for the ship to make a few trips before needing to be recharged. How to recharge it while in use, however, presented a challenge. Time was an issue. The ferry has about ten minutes between trips, and fully charging the batteries takes much longer. Moreover, plugging the ship in to the local power grid during the day would strain the system. As Odd Moen, an engineer involved in the project, explains:

> We want to recharge the batteries at the docks after each trip. Still, this will give the ferry operator only ten minutes for recharging while passengers and vehicles disembark. The problem is that the power grid in the region is relatively weak, as it was designed to provide electricity only to small villages. Briefly consuming so much energy from the medium-voltage system to recharge the ferry batteries would cause the washing machines in all the houses in the area to stop running. Obviously we can't do that to the residents here.[24]

Eventually, the researchers came up with a simple solution: They put a lithium-ion battery on each of the piers on either end of the ferry's route. When the ferry stops at either pier, the battery there supplies it with energy. While the ferry is at sea, the dockside batteries slowly regain energy from the local grid in a method known as trickle charging, which involves applying a very low continuous current to a battery, thereby avoiding overloading the grid. At night, when the ferry stops operating and the demand for electric power from local communities is at its lowest, the ship's batteries are recharged directly from the grid. A small building about the size of a newsstand houses the charging station. "Under the prevailing conditions, it was the only feasible way of building and operating a battery-powered ferry," Moen explains. "Otherwise we would have had to expand the entire grid, and that would not have been possible due to the high costs of such a project."[25]

The ferry is very quiet and produces no pollutants or greenhouse gases. It is also lightweight because it is made of aluminum rather than steel. In fact, even though the vessel carries heavy batteries, along with up to 360 passengers and 120 vehicles, it weighs about half as much as a conventional ferry. And because aluminum resists corrosion better than steel, it does not need special paint or maintenance to keep it from becoming rusted. As a result, its design helps reduce operating costs while increasing the vessel's energy efficiency and speed.

The developers hope that other electric ferries using the same technology will replace conventional ferries in fifty other short-distance routes that connect villages along Norway's fjords. Such a change would improve the air quality in coastal communities.

Harnessing the Wind

Other scientists are looking to the wind, in combination with engines fueled with alternative fuels like biogas or liquefied natural gas, to power marine vessels. Sailors have used wind to propel their ships for centuries. But the state-of-the-art wind-powered ships being developed today are quite different from those of the past.

One of the most innovative concepts is a futuristic-looking container ship known as the Vindskip. Created by Lade AS, a Norwegian company, the Vindskip is extremely aerodynamic. It has a high, sleek hull that looks like and serves as a giant sail. The ship's designer, Terje Lade, says that the ship is actually more like an airplane than a traditional cargo ship.

The Vindskip's unique shape takes advantage of apparent wind, which is the wind a ship generates as it moves. When the Vindskip sets out to sea, it uses an onboard electric engine fueled

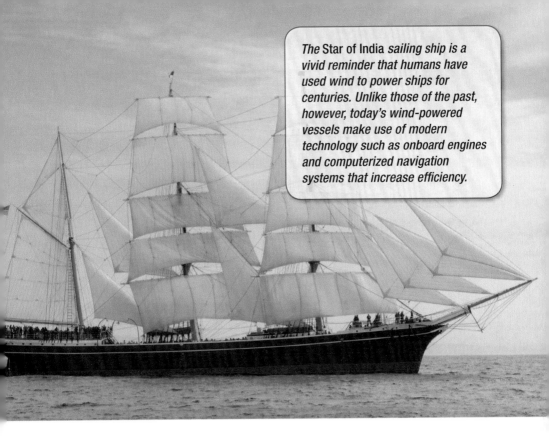

The **Star of India** *sailing ship is a vivid reminder that humans have used wind to power ships for centuries. Unlike those of the past, however, today's wind-powered vessels make use of modern technology such as onboard engines and computerized navigation systems that increase efficiency.*

by natural gas to propel it until it reaches a predetermined speed based on the wind's direction and velocity. When it reaches that speed, in much the same way that an airplane lifts off the ground, apparent wind lifts the vessel. Then, apparent wind and regular wind propel the ship toward its destination. Lade AS estimates that this system should be able to power the ship for at least 45 percent of a journey.

When the Vindskip is being propelled by the wind, the on-board engine is turned off. The engine is turned back on when wind power is not available. An onboard computer with specialized software is another part of this system. Its job is to analyze information from weather satellites about wind velocity and direction. Using this data and GPS algorithms or math formulas, it calculates the best route for the ship to take in order to optimize wind power. Among the information the software provides is data on the speed the ship must maintain throughout the voyage to best use wind power and when it is necessary to switch to engine power to reach this speed. As Lade explains, "With this software,

From Theory to Practice: Aerodynamics

The Dragon personal submarine depends on the principles of aerodynamics to allow it to travel underwater. Aerodynamics is concerned with the forces of lift and thrust. Lift is caused by air flowing over a wing. The shape of a wing determines how well air flowing over it generates lift. In an airplane the wings are shaped so that airflow around the wing creates greater air pressure on the lower half of the wing than on the upper half. This generates lift. In the case of the mini submarine, the wings are shaped so that airflow around the upper half of the wing creates greater air pressure than on the lower part of the wing. This generates negative lift, sending the vessel downward. Once underwater, the submarine's engine provides enough thrust to counteract drag and propel the vehicle forward.

you input when you want to leave and when you want to arrive, the weather forecast is loaded into the program and then it calculates the best route. This would be dynamically updated every day. At each waypoint it would check with the time arrival and tell the crew whether to speed up using the engines or slow down; it makes it very easy for the crew."[26]

Lade AS hopes to have the first Vindskip in operation by 2019. The company predicts the ship's engine will use 60 percent less fuel and generate 80 percent fewer emissions than conventional cargo ships. In fact, it is indeed possible that in the future all cargo ships will be modeled after the Vindskip.

Supersonic Submarines

While ships and boats carry goods and passengers on top of the water, submarines carry sailors, scientists, marine salvage professionals, and marine explorers underwater. In the future, submarines may welcome other travelers. Supersonic submarines now in development may someday become an alternative form of long-distance travel. In fact, Chinese scientists are looking into building a submarine that can go from Shanghai to San Francisco in less than two hours, traveling at about 3,600 miles per hour (5,794 kph).

Supersonic vehicles travel at speeds that exceed the speed of sound (Mach 1), which at sea level is about 768 miles per hour (1,236 kph). Creating a vehicle that can travel underwater at such a high speed is problematic. The drag from the water a submarine travels through slows its movement considerably. To solve this problem, the Chinese scientists are looking to supercavitation technology. Supercavitation involves creating an almost frictionless bubble around the submarine, which counteracts the drag of the water. The bubble is made of gas that is released from a nozzle on the submarine's tip. The gas envelops the vessel, allowing the water to flow around it without creating drag and slowing its movement. Supercavitation technology has already been tested on torpedoes launched from submarines.

Although supercavitation solves one problem, it presents others. Steering and maneuvering the submarine within the bubble is a major issue. Conventional submarines are controlled with a rudder, which the supersonic vessel lacks. Another issue involves creating the bubble, which can form only at a minimum speed of 62 miles per hour (100 kph). It is tricky for a submarine to reach this speed when it is first launched. The researchers, however, think they have discovered a solution to both these problems. They have developed a type of liquid skin that would be continuously sprayed out of nozzles on the submarine,

supercavitation

The forming of a bubble around a submarine or torpedo that greatly reduces underwater drag.

coating its outer surface. The liquid skin reduces friction or drag at low speeds, which would help the submarine reach a speed at which the supercavitating bubble could form. Moreover, varying the amount of fluid that is sprayed on different parts of the submarine at any given time would make it possible for more drag to be applied to one side of the craft than the other. This would create a steering effect. Although other details about the proposed submarine have not been disclosed, the concept has great potential.

Personal Submarines

While supersonic submarines promise to move travelers at speeds faster than a jet airplane, mini submarines are being developed to allow people to sightsee underwater. Personal, or mini, submarines are submersible vehicles designed to allow people to experience, explore, and appreciate underwater life. As inventor and founder of Hawkes Ocean Technologies Graham Hawkes explains: "We are going to go explore the oceans. We are going to give access. We have to because until we do, we don't understand the planet."[27]

Hawkes's firm is in the forefront of this technology. The company has developed a range of personal submarines that, unlike earlier submersible craft, do not need a mother ship to supply them with power or air. Hawkes's mini submarines are autonomous. They look more like small fighter jets than conventional submarines, and they operate using the principles of air flight. The cigar-shaped two-person submersible vessels have two pairs of wings that function like those on an airplane. One pair of wings is located in the front of the vessel and the other in the back. Both sets of wings are shorter than an airplane's wings and are inverted, so that rather than lifting the vessel upward like an airplane's wings do, the wings provide negative lift, pushing the vessel downward.

ballast

A heavy material like sand that is used to improve a vehicle's stability.

Conventional submarines use ballast tanks that are alternately filled with air or water to make the submarine dive or rise, but the radical new design of these personal submarines, combined with an electric propulsion system and thrusters (propulsion devices built into the front and back of the vessel), allow the craft to dive without ballast. Just as an airplane must reach a certain speed on the ground before being able to rise, the craft must reach a certain speed on the surface of the water before it can dive. An onboard electric motor provides the power. Once the required speed is reached, the pilot uses a joystick to steer the craft downward. In contrast to traditional submarines that are highly complex to operate, the designers made a point of creating a vessel that is simple to run.

A submersible vehicle developed by British inventor Graham Hawkes is launched in the Bahamas. The craft operates using the principles of air flight, which is why it resembles an airplane rather than a traditional submarine.

All the vessels are buoyant, meaning they cannot submerge or sink unless the propulsion system and thrusters are engaged. Once the craft submerges, if an emergency arises and the vessel loses power, it is equipped with a cutting edge safety system that automatically sends it back up to the surface. As in an airplane, the air in the cabin is pressurized so that the pilot and passenger do not have to deal with changes in air pressure.

The Dragon, the company's newest vessel, has an additional feature. Not only can it maneuver underwater, it can hover. This allows people on board to stop and look more closely at ocean life. Specialized software that regulates six propellers gives the Dragon the stability and precise movement essential to hovering, and underwater-safe lithium-ion batteries provide it with six hours of power without needing to be charged.

Personal submarines are very expensive, but their development may lead to increased ocean exploration and a greater understanding of marine life. They and other cutting edge marine vessels and technology will likely help preserve the environment and provide people with new and faster ways to travel, thereby taking an old form of transport and making it new.

CHAPTER FIVE

Aircraft and Spacecraft

In October 2015 Walmart Stores Inc. applied to the Federal Aviation Administration (FAA) for permission to test an unmanned aerial vehicle, or drone, in airspace around one of the company's buildings. The retailer wants to use drones to deliver merchandise to customers at their homes and to pickup points in store parking lots. Amazon and Google want to use drones for similar purposes. In fact, Amazon says that it expects to be ready to begin delivering packages to customers via drones as soon as federal rules permit.

Drones

Drones are robotic aircraft. They do not need a pilot inside them to fly. Some drones have a wingspan of more than 100 feet (30 m), while others can fit in the palm of a person's hand. Some drones look like miniature helicopters, while others resemble airplanes. Many are semiautonomous, meaning that a pilot who may be hundreds of miles away controls the craft, using a computer to send commands to it by means of a satellite link. The drone transmits information back to the pilot in the same way. Other drones operate without a human pilot. These autonomous aircraft carry out preprogrammed flights under the control of an onboard computer using GPS coordinates.

Highly sophisticated drones are already in use by the military for reconnaissance, surveillance, and weapons delivery missions. Law enforcement and transportation agencies are looking into using the vehicles for tasks like surveying accidents, fires, and other emergency situations and examining infrastructure like roads, bridges, and pipelines for weaknesses. Depending on the particular aircraft, drones can hover above potentially hazardous areas and take photographs and video for up to twenty-four hours, which could assist investigators.

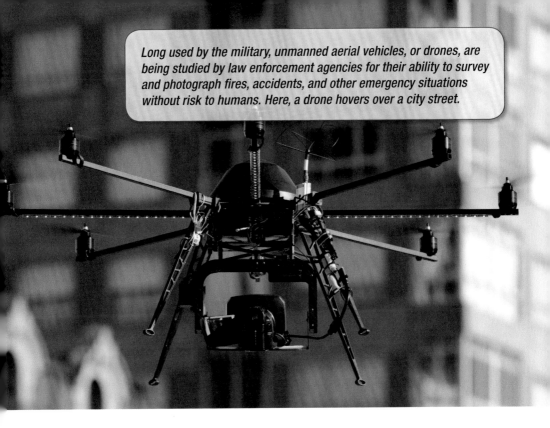

In fact, PRENAV, a California-based firm, has recently developed an autonomous drone system designed to inspect large vertical structures like cell phone towers. In the past it was almost impossible for a drone to get close to such a structure without an experienced pilot precisely navigating the craft—but not anymore. To ensure precision, instead of a human operator, the drone is controlled by a robot on the ground. "Using drones to inspect structures such as cell towers and wind turbines typically requires an expert pilot because GPS isn't adequate for close proximity flight," says Nathan Schuett, CEO of PRENAV. "The PRENAV system . . . will enable these types of missions to be performed autonomously, where the flight is aided by a robot on the ground."[28]

Before the drone is launched, a guidance robot scans the area around the structure and records the findings. A computer in the robot uses the information to produce a map of the area and a three-dimensional flight path for the drone. Once the drone takes off, the robot tracks the aircraft, sending it navigation information generated by the computer to keep it on course. Upon reaching

Drones and the Law

Drones are so new that rules and regulations concerning their use are still being developed. According to the FAA, "Unmanned aircraft systems (UAS) are inherently different from manned aircraft. Introducing UAS into the nation's airspace is challenging for both the FAA and aviation community, because the U.S. has the busiest, most complex airspace in the world. The FAA is taking an incremental approach to safe UAS integration."

In fact, the FAA planned to have rules related to the use of commercial drones ready sometime in 2016 or later. These rules would apply only to unmanned aircraft that weigh a maximum of 55 pounds (25 kg). It is not yet legal to fly larger commercial drones in US airspace. The rules would limit commercial drone flights to daylight hours and would also require that the pilot or an independent visual observer maintain a visual line of sight with the drone at all times. The rules were expected to deal with operator certification, aircraft registration and marking, and operational limits as well.

Federal Aviation Administration, "Unmanned Aircraft Systems," April 22, 2016. www.faa.gov.

its destination, the drone takes pictures of the structure that are transmitted back to the robot and converted to a model of the structure for specialists to study.

Some companies are developing drone delivery systems. In March 2016 one San Francisco–based company, Zipline International, tested a system designed to deliver medical supplies and blood to remote areas. As part of the test, an autonomous drone was sent skyward via a launching device using compressed air. GPS and special software guided it to its destination. When the drone reached the designated drop-off area, a door opened at the bottom of the craft, and a small package attached to a little parachute was released.

The company planned to use the system to deliver medical supplies to rural health facilities in Rwanda in 2016. In support of the project, the Rwandan government planned to build a network of drone ports. The drone ports, the first of their kind, will serve as drone airports. There, batteries will be recharged, drones will undergo repairs, and cargo will be loaded on and off the vehicles. If all goes as planned, the drone ports should be operational by 2020.

Other innovators are developing drones that rarely need to land or be recharged. These drones have an electric motor powered by solar energy. The Solara 50 is an example. The brainchild of New Mexico–based Titan Aerospace, this giant drone has a wingspan of 164 feet (50 m). It is designed to fly at an altitude of 65,000 feet (19,812 m), which puts it above any weather that might block out the sun.

> **hypersonic**
>
> **Speed greater than five times the speed of sound.**

More than three thousand photovoltaic cells cover the drone's wings and are intended to collect more than enough power to keep the aircraft flying during the day. Lithium-ion batteries in the wings store unused solar energy, which will power the drone at night. A small electric motor allows the aircraft to reach speeds up to 60 miles per hour (97 kph). The Solara 50 should be able to stay aloft for five years before having to land for routine maintenance.

The giant drone will be equipped with wireless communication equipment, which the craft will use to monitor weather, relay communications, patrol borders, and act as a supplement to current GPS satellites. As a matter of fact, the developers refer to the craft as an atmospheric satellite because, like a satellite, it can stay aloft for years and perform many of the same functions. However, the Solara 50 is reusable and costs much less than a satellite to build.

Beyond Supersonic Airplanes

Other innovators are looking into building supersonic and hypersonic airplanes. Supersonic aircraft are vehicles that can travel at speeds that exceed the speed of sound (Mach 1). Supersonic speeds include speeds up to Mach 5. Speeds greater than Mach 5 (about 3,800 mph or 6,100 kph) are referred to as hypersonic.

Supersonic aircraft were first developed in the middle of the twentieth century, and the military has a number of supersonic airplanes in use. But there are no commercial supersonic airplanes in operation. For a time, the Concorde, a supersonic jet, carried passengers between London or Paris and New York in three and a half hours, about half as long as a trip on a traditional jet. However, for multiple reasons, the Concorde is no longer operating. Environmental issues were a concern: The aircraft burned about 4,800 gallons (18,170 L) of fossil fuel per hour, and it produced intense noise pollution in the form of a sonic boom. A very loud noise that can harm human hearing, a sonic boom is created by shock waves that are produced when an object travels through air faster than the speed of sound. According to the National Aeronautics and Space Administration (NASA), "Air reacts like a fluid to supersonic objects. As objects travel through the air, the air molecules are pushed aside with great force. This force forms a shock wave. . . . The shock wave forms a cone of pressurized air. A sharp release of pressure after the buildup of a shock wave is heard as a sonic boom."[29]

Despite the Concorde's problems, NASA and a number of aerospace companies, including Lockheed Martin, Boeing, and Airbus, are looking into developing ultrafast airplanes. They are using new technology to create fast, quiet, environmentally friendly aircraft designed to fly at hypersonic or near hypersonic speeds. Airbus's jet, for example, is expected to reach speeds of Mach 4.5, which means it could fly between London and New York in one hour.

The jet is powered by three different kinds of engines that work in sequence. Two turbojet engines, located under the jet's body, and a rocket engine, located in the rear of the aircraft, get the aircraft off the ground. But unlike other airplanes, the jet is designed to take off vertically like a rocket. Just before the vehicle reaches Mach 1, the turbo engines turn off and retract into the aircraft's body. The rocket engine propels the jet to a cruising altitude of more than 10,000 feet (3,048 m), at which point the rocket engine also shuts off and retracts. A ramjet engine then takes over. A ramjet engine has no major moving parts. It works

SpaceX Rocket Lands on a Marine Drone

On April 8, 2016, a SpaceX rocket successfully achieved a vertical landing atop a specially created unmanned marine vessel located in the Atlantic Ocean. Before coming back to Earth, the rocket delivered a cargo ship to the International Space Station. Astronauts on the space station used a robotic arm to capture the cargo ship, which held about 7,000 pounds (3,175 kg) of freight. Among the cargo was an inflatable pod that is designed to serve as a small bedroom for astronauts when it is filled with air and attached to the space station in the future.

SpaceX was hired by NASA to deliver the cargo. But its marine landing was part of a test conducted by the spaceflight company. This was the first time this type of landing was successfully performed; four previous attempts by SpaceX failed. Since the rockets are traditionally launched over the ocean, the easiest and most fuel-efficient place to land them is out in the ocean. Being able to land a reusable rocket at sea is important because in many cases returning rockets do not have enough fuel on board to land on the ground. Carrying extra fuel for use in landing adds extra weight to a rocket, which impacts the aircraft's performance and the cost of a mission.

by sucking in outside air, which is compressed and rammed into a combustion chamber. This generates the thrust the aircraft needs to travel at near hypersonic speeds. The developers plan to use various forms of hydrogen to power the different engines, which will reduce emissions.

The best way to solve the sonic boom issue, however, has not been determined. According to Airbus, the aircraft's design, which features delta-shaped, or triangular, wings (as opposed to straight wings), combined with the location of its engines, should improve airflow over the aircraft. As a result, the shock wave should be less intense, thereby reducing the noise level. Other aeronautics companies and NASA are also investigating and testing different devices and technology that could be used to reduce sonic boom.

It may be some time before ultrafast and quiet aircraft zip passengers around the globe at near hypersonic speeds. But new technology makes the concept a realistic possibility. In fact, it is possible that by the middle of this century, such aircraft may be commercially viable.

Flying Cars

Other vehicles in the works seem more like objects ripped from movie screens than real aircraft. Flying cars are a staple of science fiction movies, not something people expect to see parked in their neighbor's garage. However, if Terrafugia, a Massachusetts-based firm, has its way, flying cars may become a common sight. The company is in the early stage of developing a flying car known as the TF-X.

The TF-X looks like a futuristic four-passenger electric automobile. It will be small enough to fit inside a single-car garage and will plug in to be recharged. When it is driven, with its wings folded into the side of the car and its propellers retracted into the vehicle's body, it will be difficult to distinguish from other cars. When it is switched to flying mode, its wings and propellers will pop up and out.

The TF-X does not need a special runway to take off. It will take off vertically from a standstill as a helicopter does. Motorized propellers lift the vehicle. This means that the TF-X can be switched from driving to flying mode almost anywhere. However, its wingspan requires 100 feet (30 meters) of clearance for takeoff and landings.

Once the craft is in the air, special propeller-like fans powered by an electric motor will provide thrust. Most of the flight will be controlled by a computer. Pilots input the destination, and an onboard computer will launch, fly, and land the vehicle. However, the pilot can override the computer when necessary.

The TF-X's electric motors make it possible for the craft to fly at a cruising speed of 200 miles per hour (322 kph) with a 500-mile (805 km) range. To reduce the vehicle's weight, it will use special tires and glass that are lighter than those used on traditional cars.

This flying vehicle is Terrafugia's forerunner of the TF-X, which is in development. On the ground, the TF-X will look much like other cars, but when it is switched to flying mode, wings and propellers will emerge from it.

Terrafugia plans to test a scale model of the TF-X in a wind tunnel soon. According to the company, "The wind tunnel test model will be used to measure drag, lift and thrust forces while simulating hovering flight, transitioning to forward flight and full forward flight."[30] If the tests prove successful, the actual vehicle will be built.

Space Travel

While some innovators are developing new aircraft to transport people and cargo on Earth, others are looking into building vehicles that take people and objects into space. One example is the *Falcon 9*, a two-stage rocket built by SpaceX, a spaceflight firm founded by Elon Musk. The *Falcon 9* was launched in December 2015. Its mission was to deliver eleven commercial satellites into orbit. Upon successfully completing the mission, the first stage of the spacecraft returned to its launch pad, landing intact in an upright position—a feat that SpaceX scientists have compared to a person balancing a broomstick in the palm of one hand. It became the first rocket in history to travel into full orbit then land back on Earth in this manner. A month earlier Blue Origin, a spaceflight firm established by Amazon founder Jeff Bezos, sent a rocket named the *New Shepard* into suborbit, which is not as high up as full orbit, and landed it vertically for reuse.

Traditionally, when a rocket returns to Earth, it either burns up upon reentry into the Earth's atmosphere or it sinks into the ocean. Since a rocket capable of space travel costs millions of dollars, creating a reusable rocket is a major step in reducing the cost of space travel. As Musk explains: "In order for us to really open up access to space, we've got to achieve full and rapid reusability. The cost to refuel our rocket—it's mostly oxygen on board—is only $200,000 to $300,000, but the cost of the rocket is $60 million."[31]

suborbital

A flight path that does not achieve the altitude or speed required to complete one full orbit of the earth.

The *Falcon 9* and *New Shepard* have different designs based on their different mission goals. The *New Shepard* is shorter and wider than the *Falcon 9*. It is designed to take space tourists about 62 miles (100 km) into space on a four-minute suborbital flight. It reaches a maximum speed of Mach 3, while the *Falcon 9* reaches Mach 7.5. The *Falcon 9* is designed to deliver and return payloads such as satellites into space and human space colonists to Mars and deeper space. It is a thin, long rocket that, when upright, is as tall as a twenty-three-story building. The *Falcon 9*'s shape helps reduce drag against the rocket as it ascends, which makes it easier for the craft to break free of the Earth's atmosphere. Conversely, its shape makes landing upright difficult, since the tall, slender rocket tends to tilt over.

From takeoff to landing, the *Falcon 9* relies on state-of-the-art technology. It is propelled upward by nine engines contained in the first stage of the rocket. The engines, which are designed to operate in a vacuum, are powered by onboard tanks of liquid oxygen and rocket-grade kerosene. When the rocket reaches an

The New Shepard *rocket is launched from a Texas facility. Unlike previous rockets, which burned up on reentry into the Earth's atmosphere, the craft is one of a new generation of reusable space vehicles.*

altitude of about 125 miles (201 km), the second stage, or booster part of the spacecraft, which is powered by another engine and which carries the payload, is released into space. Thrusters on the top of the first-stage rocket turn it from a horizontal to a vertical position. The thrusters, combined with four small heat-resistant wings known as grid fins, steer the craft down to Earth. The fins are folded into the rocket when it takes off and pop out in an X-shaped configuration around the rocket when the craft begins its descent.

As the *Falcon 9* plummets downward, the fins' waffle-like design creates small whirlwinds in the air around them. Each fin can be rotated independently, making it possible to use the vortices to help control and maneuver the vehicle. As the rocket gets closer to the ground, the rocket engines decelerate, and legs made of carbon fiber deploy. All of these systems are preprogrammed before the flight. However, a computer in the rocket constantly receives

payload

Income-producing cargo carried by a vehicle.

real-time data concerning the flight and can adjust the program and the systems as needed.

With the development of newer and newer cutting edge technology, space tourism and colonization may become a reality. As Brian Tillotson, a space travel specialist with Boeing, says: "You might see something that looks like an airplane heading to the moon or even further out. We expect to have business travelers making the trip at first, but further down the line, we'll see grandparents visiting their grandchildren."[32] Indeed, future aircraft, marine vessels, and motor vehicles will no doubt make traveling on Earth and beyond faster, cleaner, and more pleasant.

Source Notes

Introduction: Changing the World

1. Quoted in Saving Communities, "The Importance of Transportation." www.savingcommunities.org.
2. Quoted in Marilyn Siderwicz, "Pushing Engineering Boundaries to Spur Infrastructure Innovation," *MIT News*, December 22, 2015. http://news.mit.edu.

Chapter One: Powering Motor Vehicles

3. Quoted in Melissa Preddy, "A Conversation with Mary Barra," *AARP Bulletin*, September 2015, p. 4.
4. Quoted in Gov.UK, "Off Road Trials for 'Electric Highways' Technology," August 11, 2015. www.gov.uk.
5. Quoted in *Future Gadgets* (blog), "Energy Storing Body Panels," October 8, 2012. http://futuretechgadgets.blogspot.com.
6. Quoted in Eric Rugell, "Toyota on Hydrogen Fuel Cell Technology: 'Simply a Better Battery,'" *TreeHugger* (blog), November 24, 2014. www.treehugger.com.
7. Quoted in *Guardian* (Manchester), "UK's First 'Poo Bus' Goes into Regular Service," March 15, 2015. www.theguardian.com.

Chapter Two: Safe and Smart Travel

8. David Friedman, "V2V: Cars Communicating to Prevent Crashes, Deaths, Injuries," US Department of Transportation, February 3, 2014. www.transportation.gov.
9. Quoted in Gridaptive, "Smart Cities: Vehicle to Infrastructure and Adaptive Roadway Lighting Communication Standards," 2012. www.gridaptive.com.
10. Bill Howard, "V2V: What Are Vehicle-to-Vehicle Communications and How Do They Work?," *ExtremeTech* (blog), February 6, 2014. www.extremetech.com.

11. Quoted in National Highway Traffic Safety Administration, "U.S. Department of Transportation Issues Advance Notice of Proposed Rulemaking to Begin Implementation of Vehicle-to-Vehicle Communications Technology," August 18, 2014. www.nhtsa.gov.
12. Quoted in David Undercoffler, "54 Million Self-Driving Cars Will Be on the Road by 2035, Study Finds," *Los Angeles Times*, January 2, 2014. http://articles.latimes.com.
13. Quoted in David Levitan, "Self-Driving Cars: Coming Soon to a Highway Near You," *Yale Environment 360*, July 23, 2012. http://e360.yale.edu.
14. Quoted in Levitan, "Self-Driving Cars."
15. Quoted in Richard Read, "NHTSA Lays Out Groundrules for Autonomous Vehicles," Car Connection, June 7, 2013. www.thecarconnection.com.
16. Quoted in Nicole Casal Moore, "U-M Opens Mcity Test Environment for Connected and Driverless Vehicles," Michigan Engineering, July 20, 2015. www.engin.umich.edu.

Chapter Three: High-Speed Public Transportation

17. Quoted in Tiffany Acosta, "NMSU Grads Helping Build Nation's First Bullet Train," *Las Cruces (NM) Sun News*, January 3, 2016, p. 2C.
18. Quoted in Jon Stewart, "Maglevs: The Floating Future of Trains?," BBC News, November 18, 2014. www.bbc.com.
19. Loz Blain, "Ultra-efficient 4,000 mph Vacuum-Tube Trains—Why Aren't They Being Built?," *Gizmag*, July 10, 2012. www.gizmag.com.
20. Evacuated Tube Transport Technologies, "Why ET3?," www.et3.com.
21. Quoted in James Vhalos, "Hyped Up: Startups Race to Bring the Hyperloop to Life," *Popular Science*, July 7, 2015. www.popsci.com.

Chapter Four: Marine Vehicles

22. Quoted in Sandia National Laboratories, "Red and White Fleet Going Green," July 27, 2015. https://share.sandia.gov.
23. Quoted in Sandia National Laboratories, "Red and White Fleet Going Green."
24. Quoted in Siemens, "Setting a Course for Carbon-Free Shipping," March 17, 2016. www.siemens.com.
25. Quoted in Siemens, "Setting a Course for Carbon-Free Shipping."
26. Quoted in Peter Shadboldt, "'Vindskip' Cargo Ship Uses Its Hull as a Giant Sail," CNN, January 16, 2015. www.cnn.com.
27. Quoted in DeepFlight, "DeepFlight Dragon: The World's Most Amazing Gift," December 2015. http://us12.campaignarchive2.com.

Chapter Five: Aircraft and Spacecraft

28. Quoted in NAW Staff, "FAA-Approved PRENAV Drone System Suited for Turbine Inspections," North American Wind Power, November 25, 2015. http://nawindpower.com.
29. National Aeronautics and Space Administration, "What Is Supersonic Flight?," May 19, 2009. www.nasa.gov.
30. Quoted in Rob Edwards, "Terrafugia's New TF-X Proves Impractical Flying Cars Are Still a Thing," TechRadar. www.techradar.com.
31. Quoted in Irene Klotz, "Why the SpaceX Rocket Ocean Landing Is a Big Deal," Discovery News, April 11, 2016. http://news.discovery.com.
32. Quoted in MSN Travel, "This Is What Air Travel Will Actually Look like in 100 Years," April 5, 2016. www.msn.com.

For Further Research

Books

Stuart Kallen, *What Is the Future of Drones?* San Diego: ReferencePoint, 2016.

Marge T. Oge, *Driving in the Future: Combating Climate Change with Cleaner, Smarter Cars.* New York: Arcade, 2015.

Louise Spilbury, *Drones.* New York: Stevens, 2016.

Louise Spilbury, *Maglev Trains.* New York: Stevens, 2016.

Stephanie Watson, *What Is the Future of Self-Driving Cars?* San Diego: ReferencePoint, 2016.

Internet Sources

Sean Cooper, "What You Need to Know About Self-Driving Cars," *Engadget* (blog), June 6, 2014. www.engadget.com/2014/06/06/explainer-self-driving-cars.

Sourav Das, "10 Cutting Edge Technologies Soon to be Used in Cars," Wonderslist. www.wonderslist.com/10-cutting-edge-technologies-soon-used-cars.

FutureforAll.org, "Future Cars," 2016. www.futureforall.org/transportation/futurecars.htm.

Seamus Payne, "Sea Spectacles: 10 Cutting Edge Boats of the Future," Coolist, 2016. www.thecoolist.com/luxury-yachts-10-amazing-yachts-of-the-future.

Websites

Gizmag (www.gizmag.com). *Gizmag* is an online magazine that publishes articles related to technology, science, and transportation.

Green Car Reports (www.greencarreports.com). This website provides lots of information about hybrid and alternative fuel vehicles.

Popular Mechanics (www.popularmechanics.com). The website of *Popular Mechanics* magazine provides a wide range of articles related to motor vehicles, air and space travel, and cutting edge transportation technology.

SpaceX (www.spacex.com). The website of the spaceflight company provides lots of information about reusable rockets.

US Department of Transportation (www.transportation.gov). The website of this government agency provides information about transportation issues and new technology and solutions.

Index

Picture Credits

About the Author

Barbara Sheen is the author of ninety-three books for young people. She lives in New Mexico with her family. In her spare time, she likes to swim, walk, garden, and cook.